When Baby Becomes Big Sibling

Paula Rollo

Table of Contents

Introduction

The huge transition from baby to big brother or big sister is a big deal! Transitions are hard on all of us, but they can be particularly difficult for our little ones. Adding a new sibling changes the entire family dynamic. This isn't a bad thing, but it is definitely a challenge.

My son was barely a year old when we found out we were expecting his sister, and he was 21 months old when she was born. I'm a huge planner (some might say control freak) by nature, so I did everything I could while I was pregnant to prepare my little guy for the arrival of his new sibling.

I read about it online, I polled other moms, and I stressed out entirely too much! After baby arrived, I kept right on planning (stressing) and doing my best to help my little boy through the hard transitions that came with bringing our new baby home.

We had some hard days that made me feel like I was failing and we had some awesome days that made me feel like a stellar mama. All in all, the transition went a lot smoother than I ever imaged it could.

I'm so grateful for the time I spent working with my son both before and after his sister's birth. I truly believe these things helped him transition as easily as possible, and I know it all helped me stay sane during the crazy times when both kids were wailing at the same time or while I was trying to figure out the brand new logistics of a grocery store trip.

It's all new and fresh, but it's pretty fun, too! I hope this book helps your transition as you add a new baby to your family, and that it encourages you to know that you can make it through.

Happy reading!

--Paula
Author of www.BeautyThroughImperfection.com

PAULA ROLLO

Section One

Preparing

Yourself

CHAPTER ONE
Pregnancy

This is definitely harder than I remember

Let me preface this by saying that if you are one of those people that loves being pregnant and you feel like Wonder Woman the entire time, I applaud you. But this chapter is not for you. If, however, you feel like a moderately-sized hippopotamus and could describe your pregnancy as a fog of weary forgetfulness and pain, please feel free to keep reading.

When I got pregnant with my son, I was a newlywed, working a part time job and involved in an internship at my church. I was a pretty busy gal, but I still found time to nap almost daily and consume twice my body weight in snack food every two hours. Pregnancy was by no means easy, but I rocked it and made it to (and past) my due date without exceeding amounts of difficulties.

Then my second pregnancy came along.

I had transitioned to a stay at home mom, so I wasn't working or interning, "just" chasing a 13 month old cutie, and wow. Thinking about those days makes me want to take a sympathy nap right now.

I can't even begin to describe the sheer exhaustion that would overwhelm me approximately 11 seconds after waking up each day. The nausea was about the same, but when it came to aches, pains, and tiredness I think everything somehow tripled in difficulty from my first pregnancy to my second.

One thing that I was not expecting at all was how difficult feeding my older child would be. Naturally, I realized that I would have to prepare food and snacks for him while nauseous. I took to holding my breath while I microwaved chicken nuggets, trying not to gag as the aroma found its way into my nose despite my best efforts.

I had foreseen this being an issue long before the nausea hit, but what I wasn't prepared for was the way my toddler would take it upon himself to feed me. As in climbing into my lap with a fist full of food and attempting to maneuver it into my mouth. I couldn't even bring myself to open my mouth to tell my son no, afraid of what might happen if I parted my lips in the slightest. Oh the joys of morning, (and by morning, I mean all day) sickness when there's already a little one to feed. While I could tell my hubby he would need to fend for himself, my toddler (obviously) could handle no such direction, and I had to endure.

As if the food fiasco wasn't enough, don't get me started on the tiredness. I actually found myself praying that my son would take an extra long nap so I could have longer to sleep as well. My bump had yet to pop when I began going to bed shortly after my husband got off work, simply because I couldn't make it any more.

Speaking of bumps, that seemed to come faster this time around, as well. Maternity clothes in the first trimester, anyone? I certainly needed them much earlier than I did with my second pregnancy.

Maybe it's because you know what is coming the second time around, but it seemed like everything happened just a little bit sooner than it did the first time. Braxton-Hicks contractions showed up in my second trimester and didn't seem to relent until a week after the baby was born.

It seemed like every month I'd lament a new ache or pain to my OB, thinking to myself *surely this isn't supposed to be happening yet,* only to have her smile sympathetically and let me know that whatever "it" was for that month was normal and that I should just get used to it.

Pregnancy #2 is no walk in the park by any stretch of the imagination, which is why I want to tell you this: don't be too hard on yourself. If you need to turn on Curious George and rest a bit, do it. You are already dividing your energy between your kiddos, and sometimes the one in your belly needs a bit of extra rest from you. That's totally okay and (dare I say it?) *normal*.

I know your raging hormones may try to tell you that you're the worst mother ever right now. Mine definitely had a few choice words to say to me on days when I put my toddler in the pack n play and slept nearby because I literally couldn't keep my eyes open anymore.

But you know what? Your hormones don't have to stay awake, so there's no way they can understand how hard this is for you. Unless those same hormones are also volunteering to cook dinner for the family, feel free to tell them to shut it, then you go take a little nap.

> "Your **hormones** don't have to stay awake, so there's no way they can **understand** how hard this is for you."

Instead of feeling guilty, try to figure out fun ways to interact with your kiddo while staying seated or even laying down. I used to lie down and tickle my boy, just so I didn't have to stand up or move around. He loved the interaction, and it helped me sneak in a few precious moments of rest. It may sound crazy, but I was taking all I could get at that point.

Save Your Sanity

Playtime. One way to incorporate resting time for you with play time for him is to buy some new puzzles to play on the ground (preferably in a horizontal position). My favorite trick is to keep some toys locked up out of reach in a closet and only pull them out when you need a break. They will be so excited about the "new" toys that they will give you a few moments of peace to catch up. I call these "closet toys," and they are how I survive life. For real.

Meal time. I have a theory that crock pots are a special little gift, specifically intended for pregnant women. You can choose the time of day in which you are least-tired and not *as* nauseous to cook. This way, the rest of your family can still have a home-cooked meal at the normal dinner hour, even if you have already been asleep for hours or can't stand the notion of being near food by 6pm.

Support systems. Another life saver? Really amazing friends. I'm not sure how I would have gotten through pregnancy number two without the incredible gals at my church, a few in particular. "Oh, we'll come over and watch your son for an hour while you take a nap," they'd say. Or, "I'll be dropping by around 5pm with dinner for your family, OK?" Seriously. You can't make up people this fantastic. I'd oblige, because I wasn't quite capable of keeping my eyes open much longer, and awaken to a spotless kitchen and scrubbed toilets.

In my hormonal-pregnant state, this usually brought tears to my eyes, both because I was so grateful and because I was secretly feeling guilty that I couldn't handle everything in the world all on my own. But I learned something, really: don't be afraid to ask for help.

Growing a baby is serious business, and sometimes we all could use a nap, or a friend that's not afraid of doing dishes. It never hurts to be that friend, either, when your girlfriends are facing pregnancies of their own. Just keep passing the love (and naps) around! Growing the baby is all on you, so don't be afraid to ask for some assistance in the things that don't have to be entirely on your shoulders.

Pregnancy is rough, but thankfully, it's only 40(ish) weeks long, and you can totally handle that. I mean, you've done it before, right? So you <u>can</u> do it again.

Even when it hurts and you can barely keep your eyes open, you've got this mama! You've got this.

Preparing Your Marriage

I don't talk about my husband a whole lot in this book, not because he isn't awesome (because he totally is), but simply because he's at work when most of my worries and fears rear their little heads. Oh, and also during 99.8% of all the toddler tantrums that I deal with on a daily basis. There's something about daddy being home that makes both kiddos (who might have been screaming their little hearts out moments earlier) turn into these adorable little cherubs who want nothing more than to cuddle quietly on the couch with their daddy while he reads them stories.

I'm not kidding. I would say it's ridiculous, but I kinda treasure that time, so I can't bring myself to speak ill of it. Watching my man with our kiddos is one of the best things ever, and well, you don't really need a chapter in a book dedicated to "prepare yourself for the best thing ever," right?

But I did think that there were a few things worth mentioning about marriage and transitioning to having yet another member of the family. I'm no marriage expert or anything, but hubby and I have been happily married for 5 years (and counting), so take this for whatever that's worth.

Talk About It – Even the Rough Stuff

If you are like me, you are probably not the most polite individual when you are pregnant. I get cranky, defensive and moody. I tend to take everything personally and expect a lot more from my husband than normal (and far more than what is fair).

A few months after my first pregnancy, I was able to see a bit more clearly that I wasn't the most pleasant person to be around while pregnant. Thankfully, my hubby took it all like a champ and loved me through it, but I knew I wanted to do better the second time.

My next pregnancy was actually harder than my first. I hurt more, I was ridiculously tired, and don't get my husband started on how cranky I was. But our marriage was a lot stronger through the second. I think this was mainly because we learned to talk things through instead of merely enduring the 40+ weeks.

When I got upset about something the second time, I could usually identify that it was my hormones messing with my head, and that my husband had not freakishly morphed into a jerk the moment I conceived our child. This didn't necessarily alleviate my moodiness, but it certainly made it easier for both of us to endure. Hubby could hug me and console me during a fit of tears, knowing that I would apologize in a few hours and tell him that my hormones were making me crazy and that I'm thankful for what a sweetie he is.

· I learned to let go of things that irritate me during pregnancy. Yes, there were several things that came up that my husband did that drove me absolutely crazy. I would think to myself, "How am I going to live with this for the rest of my life?! I need to say something! This has to stop!" And then I would take a breather, keep my mouth shut, and decide to hold off on the conversations about my pet peeves for after my pregnancy.

I'm glad I did, because honestly, I couldn't care less about those things now that my hormones aren't taking over my brain. Is it really that big of a deal for me to pick up some extra laundry sometimes or occasionally change the toilet paper roll myself if he forgets? Nope. It's really not. So unless it's actually a major marriage issue, you might want to consider waiting until a few months AFTER baby to discuss it. Let your hormones fizzle out a bit before you question his love for you over dirty socks, toilet paper, or a nearly empty gas tank.

Learning to talk things through has been a huge relief for our marriage. We would try to set times when my hormones were at their happiest, then take that opportunity to talk about things that really mattered. This seems to work best for us with a bowl of chocolate ice cream in hand, but who am I to say what will work for you.

Eat a carton of ice cream, and then ask your husband what the hardest parts of your last pregnancy were for him. Keep in mind he's not telling you what you are doing wrong; he's sharing what's been hard for *him*. **Don't let your hormones tell you that you are failing**! Just use it as a learning experience to try to help make the situation easier for him by focusing on fixing the things that are hardest on him, even if it means letting go of something else.

You can share your hardships, as well, and then brainstorm ways you can help each other through the hard spots. For my husband, it was my emotional outbursts. So, we figured out a way for me to communicate: "I'm not really mad at you, but my hormones are making me feel unloved" or something similar…then he could hold me and comfort me, without feeling as if he needed to defend his actions.

Have the same discussion about the newborn stage of life. See if you can make a plan now to help the transitions go easier on the whole family once the baby arrives. Remember that you are in this *together*. As crazy as things may get, you can rely on one another! Just keep the lines of communication OPEN. Even if that means saying "my hormones are really mad at you right now, so I need a big hug!" or "I need some alone time. You don't need to change anything; I'm just upset about something that doesn't really matter, because I'm pregnant." Saying something like that will buy you some time to work through it without making it a long-term problem in your marriage.

Oh, the Hormones

Speaking of hormones, I would just like to give props to all the dads who lovingly endure the hormonal ups and downs of their wives' pregnancies.

Let's be honest, hormones are just plain rough. They are hard on every one. The woman that's producing them, the children that have to endure hormonal mama, and the husband that has to live with a ragingly hormonal wife. Can we be honest and just say it's a challenge for us all?

My poor husband has had to put up with more than his fair share of hormonal-wife days. Something about pregnancy always tends to hit me hard, and I become a wee bit irrational (shhhh, don't tell him I said that...or maybe do tell him, since he deserves a pat on the back for enduring 20 months by my side while the hormones morphed me into monster-wifey).

The thing is, men can't understand it because they've never been there. They don't have the same emotional swings that we do, and they can certainly never experience pregnancy. So when we start tearing up over the way little Johnny blinked tonight or become hurt at the sound of anything less than pure glee in regard to tonight's dinner selection, I doubt they can quite comprehend, much less keep up.

Pregnancy can be a trying time on a marriage *for both parties*. I remember constantly doubting my husband's love for me. Not because he had changed anything at all, but because I had. I was more needy and required constant reassurance and a large number of hugs. I'm sure, at times, it was probably insulting to him that I would ask "Do you love me?" an obnoxious amount of times during the week, but that was just my hormones raging and I needed to be reminded. A lot.

There may be certain things that you need to discuss. If he gets hurt that you are questioning his love for you 100 times a day, maybe you can try to tone it down a bit, and he can try to remind you a few extra times throughout the day. Find simple solutions to things that are big problems. And I'm confident that there are simple solutions, because most of it wouldn't even be a big problem if your hormones weren't raging (don't hate me for admitting it out loud).

CHAPTER TWO
Stresses and Concerns

But I can barely keep up with one!

Do you ever find yourself rubbing your preggo belly while watching your older child spinning around you, destroying everything in his wake… and just want to cry?

I remember one day, as I was sprinting across the playground, clutching my nine-month pregnant belly (all 70 extra pounds of it), chasing my one-year-old, thinking *what in the world have I gotten myself into???*

I feel like toddlers should automatically become slower and less energetic whenever their mothers conceive, but unfortunately the opposite seems to be true. The kiddos have even more energy and become even feistier than ever before.

It can be downright terrifying at times thinking about having two children running around, but I will let you

25

in on a little secret: *the baby won't be able to run right away.*

Sure, that may be obvious, but it's nice to remember. Your child won't emerge from the womb as a tantrum-throwing mess of a toddler. It will be a tiny newborn, and it will pretty much just lay there for a few months to give your body (and sanity) time to catch up.

Yes, a year or two from now the new baby will be out there running with the best of them, but by that time your older child will have grown and matured, too.

A lot happens in the development of a child over a year. Remember that, and take a deep breath. You are already a great mama for your little one, and you will be a great mama again.

We are all just figuring it out as we go, and you already have a few years/months of figuring it out under your belt. You've been rocking this motherhood thing for a while now, and you can definitely handle one more!

What If I Don't Love This One as Much as I Love My First?

This fear literally kept me up at night. In fact, all of my sleepiness that first trimester could largely be attributed to the lack of sleep I was getting at night because I would lie awake worrying!

I love my son so much. How could I not? He's my kid! The love I feel for him can't be explained in words, pictures, or any other method of communication. It's just not possible.

I was terrified that I would not be able to feel that level of connection and love for another human. How could this passion and love be duplicated? How could my heart that was already full of love, so much that it hurt, contain that much adoration for another tiny baby?

I can't truthfully explain how it works, how the heart of a mama grows and increases with each new baby, but it happens. I can't describe it. I don't love my babies the same way, but I love them the same amount.

The blood that flows through my veins beats for both of them now, not just my first, and it always will.

The blood that flows through my veins beats for both of them now, not just my first, and it always will. Without sacrificing any of the love I had for my son, my heart bursts with love for my baby girl.

It's like magic, and I'm so thankful for it.

My first week with the princess was a time of us growing together, and I could feel my love for her increasing every time I looked at her, touched her and smelled her. It was still magic, though a different type than I felt in the first 20 seconds of my son's life.

Two different children, two different experiences, but one love that we share. I can't explain how it comes to pass; I can just tell you that it does.

If you don't feel that magic immediately, don't let it scare you (more on that later). Take time to notice the love growing as you kiss and rock that new baby, and you will feel it. You will know that you are once again a part of something amazing. You are the mother of new life, and it will be magical.

Am I a Good-Enough Mom to Handle Another?

It was sort of ironic that none of these fears came up in my mind until *after* I was already pregnant. Maybe it had to do with the hormones, or perhaps it was just that I was actually preparing to mother another child, instead of just "hoping to get pregnant," but for some reason, dozens of worries and fears came from every direction shortly after I saw the two lines on my HPT.

One of my biggest worries was definitely, "Am I a good enough mama to handle another one?"

You see, my son hit a particularly difficult toddler stage in the middle of my pregnancy with his sister. He was throwing tantrums about virtually everything in life, and you could frequently find him screaming, kicking me, or throwing something in the general direction of my face.

This was not an easy time for an already exhausted pregnant mama, and it definitely left me wondering about my parenting skills and whether I would indeed be worthy of mothering another child.

My husband shared a bit of wisdom with me in this season that always helps me whenever I think about it. He said: *"Just the fact that you are worrying about it should tell you that you are a good mom. Bad moms don't worry about whether they are doing a good job."*

Naturally, a lack of worry isn't a cause for concern, but it did comfort my heart a bit to think about it that way. I am doing my best, and big brother is learning and growing up pretty well.

Sure, there are tantrums and LOTS of hard days, but he's a kid and I'm a mom. I'm pretty sure that just comes with the territory. The thing about being a good enough mama is that I don't think I ever will be. I don't feel worthy of these kids at all -- just extremely thankful that I have been chosen to be their mama.

Unrelentingly, I'm trusting in God that He will enable me to mother them in a way that points them to Him and allows them to feel loved and cared for all of their days. Because when it comes down to it, I've given up on trying to be the perfect mama. I'm just trying to be a loving mama.

Sometimes, that means I'm a bit stricter than I would like to be, because I know they need to learn from whatever naughtiness just occurred. Sometimes, that means I don't let it get to me when they spoon applesauce into the back pocket of my jeans while I'm wearing them (true story, by the way) because I know they just wanted to see what it would be like.

Sometimes, it means I fail. But it always means that I end the day by kissing their faces and thanking God for another day of life with them.

As mothers, we make mistakes every day, and we always will. No matter what we do or how we do it, there will always be people telling us we're doing it wrong while others are singing our praises.

I have come to realize that as hard as I try to raise my kids the best way that I know how, they will probably look back on their childhoods and see things that they will do differently with their kids. And that's okay. It doesn't mean that I'm not cut out for this or not worthy of being a mama of more than one.

It just means I'm a mother, a mother who loves my kiddos fiercely and loves them so much that I stay up at night worrying about how I can love them more. It's just how mothers are wired, to love and to stress. But the more we can drop the stress part, the more we can find joy and peace in the midst of the craziness and chaos that seems to multiply with each additional kiddo.

So in answer to the question, "Am I ready for another kid?" I would ask another: "Is anyone ever ready?" How could you ever be fully prepared to care for the life and well-being of another precious human life?

There's no schooling or book that can tell you the answer to that question, and there is no quiz or 5-step program that can gauge your readiness as a parent. You just kinda have to decide to take the leap before you even think you are ready, because there is no secret to being "ready" at all. Sometimes, the leap is taken for you with a little surprise "positive!"

Either way, I've learned that the key is to focus less on your skill set as a mama and more on how you can love your children and show them the love of Christ. Truly, our most important job is to feed them physically, emotionally, and spiritually, not to be the coolest mama on the block.

It's a tall order, but it's one that we can accomplish. It's one that we have been chosen by God to accomplish, so whatever your fears, insecurities, and worries, know that God will equip you when the time is right.

Whatever your fears, insecurities, and worries, know that God will equip you when the time is right.

It won't necessarily be easy, but we're never promised easy, no matter how long we wait (or planned to wait) to have another child. It will always be a challenge. But it's one that can be conquered with love.

Drop those stresses at the door, mama, because you may not be a world-class chef or the best storyteller. Maybe you can't carry a lullaby tune in a bucket, or perhaps you are like me and you absolutely *loathe* breastfeeding.

In the end, none of those things really matter. *Your love matters,* and I bet you are pretty stellar at loving your kids, which makes you an incredible mama to one kid or twenty.

This Will be Hard. *And Awesome.*

I'm not going to lie to you, this is going to be difficult. Is there are part of motherhood that is not?

Yes, there will be days when you will have "*What was I thinking having children in the first place?!*" thoughts, and then you'll probably be plagued with guilt for even letting such questions enter your mind. I know; I've totally been there. Like yesterday. And I probably will be there next week, too.

Motherhood isn't a cake walk (though a little cake here and there does help!). There are going to be hard days. There will be times when both kids are screaming at the exact same time and you just want to go hide under a nice, warm blanket instead of trying to decipher what the tantrums and the tears are all about.

You know why? Because you are a mom. You are just one person. Please, I beg of you, don't be too hard on yourself. We all have hard days. Every last one of us.

In fact, think of the best mom that you know. The one that you look at and go "Wow! If I could be half as cool a mom as her, I'd be doing pretty good." Think about her life, and recognize that *she has hard days, too.*

Every single good mom on the planet has had a bad day. Every last one of us. So when the hard days come and you feel like you are losing it, just take it in stride and realize that you are part of a very inclusive club of good mothers who also have hard days.

Keep something in mind for me, would you? Remember that you are awesome. And most of all, that your awesomeness as a parent is not dependent upon the number of tantrums your child does or does not throw in a day.

You are not shunned from the "good moms club" whenever your toddler has an off day or even when you accidentally let the newborn fuss for 15 minutes before feeding him in the middle of the night because you'd already been up half the night with a sick toddler and didn't hear the baby until your husband woke you up to feed him. (This is another true story, by the way. This totally happened in our house. More than once.) Every one lives through it. You are not a bad mom for any of those things.

And all the tantrums and regression that your older kiddo is probably about to go through? All of that is *completely normal.* An absolutely ordinary part of childhood and not a cause for alarm or guilt.

Just keep going. There will be some days that you are the awkward parent standing in the middle of the grocery store with multiple wailing children, not daring to get out of line, because you know they won't stop and you really have to buy food for the family to eat (another true story, if you're wondering). But then there will be other days that you'll be the one with the perfectly little angel of a toddler who is standing with you in line singing lullabies to the tiny infant who is starting to drift off to sleep in the baby carrier. Just try to smile encouragingly at the mom with the screaming kiddos whenever you get to be the mom with the quiet ones, and we'll all turn out okay.

This is a roller coaster ride. Just like the last few months/years of motherhood already have been.

But there is something beautiful and awesome in every day. Take the time to see it. Even if you have to sneak into your kids' rooms after they've been out for awhile to kiss their foreheads and remember what a precious gift that they are. Do it. Remind yourself on the hard days that every day won't be hard. In fact, you have some awesome and ridiculously fun days ahead, too.

But I'm getting ahead of myself...

CHAPTER THREE
Birth...Again

What was I thinking?

For some of us, the mere thought of giving birth again is enough to invoke an intense feeling of dread. My first birth did not go as planned. It was quick but severe as I went from four cm dilation to holding my baby in less than an hour.

While those who can boast being in labor for days on end probably think an hour sounds glorious, let me just put it out there that no one really wins in this situation. I truly can't imagine enduring active labor for 12+ hours the way that my friends have done, but then I had all my pain compacted and shoved into one vicious hour. So, again. There's no winning. Just pain, mainly, and the wonder of having a baby.

When my husband asked me later to describe to him

what labor and delivery felt like, the only term that seemed to come close was what I whispered quietly to him: *"Death. It felt like death, honey."* Amazing that it takes the feeling of dying to bring new life into the world, but that's a topic for another time.

What I want to discuss here is that each birth is unique and beautiful in it's own way. If your first birth didn't go quite like you wanted it to, don't let that increase your worry for this one. No matter how many children you have, it's different every time. And, thankfully it doesn't last forever. One day of agony is nothing compared to the month of painful pregnancy or the years of joy with your child.

I had hoped to have a medication-free birth with my son, but I ended up changing my tune mid-labor in the hospital as I screamed at my doula to go get a nurse right this very minute and give me SOMETHING in my IV. *Just make it stop!!!!*

With my daughter, I had a much less rigid birth plan. I wanted to try again for no pain-meds, but I wasn't all that concerned about taking them if I felt I needed them. She ended up coming so quickly that I couldn't have had any relief, even if I had wanted it.

In fact, she made her debut 5 minutes after we arrived at the hospital, and mere seconds after my husband came running into the delivery room after parking the car. My birth plan didn't even make past the parking lot at our hospital. So much for thinking ahead! Despite the fact that I almost delivered her in the brand new car that we had purchased 3 days prior, it was a much easier birth and I was relieved to be done as quickly as I was.

Both of my births were quick. The first time, I was induced in the hospital, and the second, she just came on her own sweet time. Daughter and son were both late, and I was severely impatient to meet them both. Some things were the same, but others were different. The only thing I can really say is that it doesn't help to be concerned. All the worry in the world won't make birth any easier, and it won't help you be prepared any more than you already are.

I am all for mamas educating themselves and making good choices about birth. Good choices as in *whatever is right for their family*. That literally looks different for everyone. Don't let someone else guilt you into feeling bad about your own decisions. At the end of the day, a beautiful baby entering the world matters far more than the methods and the concerns that we mothers fret about for months upon end.

Every birth is as different as the child it brings into the world. There is no "cheating" or "winning" at childbirth. It's hard on all of us, regardless of the choices we make in the delivery room, or even where we choose for our delivery room to be! Vaginal birth, medications or the lack thereof, c-section, homebirth, or a birthing center. All are great choices for different families. Do what is right for you and this baby. Don't let fear of how last time went keep you from embracing this birth experience as best you can.

Whichever way your precious one enters the world, it will be awesome, and you are awesome. There is no "cheating" at birth; that's not possible. You are birthing a baby, an entire human being. It's a wonderful (painful) gift we've been given as women. Regardless of the method you choose or the method that is chosen for you, it's awe inspiring. It's your birth story, and it is beautiful.

The Guilt-Monster of Bonding

There is much debate about which is the best birthing method. I've seen many mommy wars waged on this very topic, as moms argue over which way is the best, hardest, healthiest, or promotes the best bond between mommy and baby.

I definitely think that it is important for moms to make informed birthing choices and to plan for what they feel will be best for them and their babies. What I don't like is when mamas start attacking each other, or trying to make others feel inferior for their birthing opinions or chosen methods.

Before my son was born, I was told that vaginal birth with no drugs is the absolute **best**. I was given multiple reasons for this, but the most common was for *bonding* with the baby. I'm sure that there have been medical studies done on the topic, though, and that's really not what I'm here to discuss. What I know for sure is that many wonderful mamas still carry guilt for their birth methods, and I know even more pregnant mamas who harbor fears that they will not be able to give birth the "right" way. I am 100% for moms making informed decisions about birth and going into it with both eyes open, *but* I'm a bit weary of the guilt trips that all-too-often accompany that information.

I am 100% for moms making informed decisions about birth and going into it with both eyes open.

But I'm a bit weary of the guilt trips that all-too-often accompany that information.

This is why I'm sharing my story:

When I was pregnant with my first baby, I made a birth plan that described all my wishes and hopes in great detail. It said I didn't want any type of medical intervention and that I wanted to deliver him vaginally without any painkillers. Nine days past my due date, I was induced, but I was still hoping to have a pain-medication-free birth. I was so worried about doing everything "right" and not being judged by people who might think that I was selfish or weak for taking pain medication.

A few hours into labor, all those hopes flew out the window, and I begged for intervention. The nurses gave me something in my IV that made me both drowsy and loopy. An hour later, my son was born. The doctor laid him on my chest, and he was the most beautiful thing I had ever seen.

I still remember the tears flowing down my cheeks as I stared at his perfect little face. I can't adequately describe the love that I felt in that moment, but it still gets me teary-eyed when I think about it. The bond I felt for my son was immediate, even with the pitocin flowing through my body, accompanied by whatever medication they gave me in that IV for the pain. It wasn't what I had planned, but it was beautiful.

*It wasn't what I had planned, but it was **beautiful.***

Then came my second birth. My birth plan didn't even make it in the building (neither did my OB). She was born in three quick pushes without even a chance to get any type of medical intervention. There were a couple issues with me afterwards, but her actual birth was pretty much perfect.

But if I'm honest, I didn't feel that immediate bond when she was placed on my chest. Instead of weeping at her beauty and being in awe of the miracle of life, I literally remember looking down on her and thinking "Eh, she's here, that's nice." That was it.

The world didn't stop turning the way it did with my son, and I don't remember crying at all. I was happy, relieved, and full of love, but it was very…different. I didn't even realize until a few hours later that the bond was not immediate with her the way it was with my son. It's hard to describe the difference in emotions, but it was definitely unique and entirely unexpected.

I mean, I had a completely medication-free birth. That's supposed to mean perfection right? The perfect birth story complete with immediate bonding? Or not. Like I said before, every single birth is unique, and the little factors that we stress about for weeks typically don't have a lasting impact for the rest of our lives as mothers and children.

After my issues were cleared up, I was able to nurse my daughter before she was taken to the nursery for her newborn tests. I stayed awake for awhile waiting on her. I wasn't exhausted the way I had been with my son, and I wanted desperately to see her, but I wasn't frantic as I had been two years earlier when my son was separated from me for his newborn tests. As I spent the first night with her, and many nights since then, our bond has grown and deepened, and it has been a beautiful process to watch.

The bond with both of my kids is equal now, but I still find it interesting when I think about it. The medicated birth that lead to an immediate bond with my son, and the easy birth with no interventions without the *immediate* bond. It goes to illustrate that every birth is truly unique and beautiful in its own way. I have no regrets about the births of either of my children. Neither went the way that I was expecting, but I smile at the memory of both.

I write this for those that worry that your birth won't be *perfect*. Birth rarely goes the way that we have planned, but each is beautiful and difficult in its own way.

Birth is not a competition, it's personal, and it is up to you (with the help of your health providers) to decide what the best method is for your family.

And to the moms who worry about bonding with their babies... It's true that it's not always immediate, *but that isn't your fault.* And it doesn't have to affect your entire relationship with your child.

My daughter will probably never know that the magical-emotional bond wasn't there immediately after her birth *(at least not until I tell her as she's preparing to birth children of her own).* She won't know because it doesn't affect our lives today, just as the choices I made during their births do not affect us today. The Pitocin, the pain medicine, and the *near birth in the car.* They each lead to the same outcome: a healthy baby welcomed into a family full of love.

The love that I feel for both of my children goes so far beyond what I felt for them in their first few days of life. It grows every day, and I doubt that it will ever stop.

So enough with the mommy-guilt -- bring on the mommy-support!. Support for all mamas, for all birthing decisions and all birth plans (even the ones that stay tucked away in the car while mama delivers the baby).

Section Two

Preparing Your Toddler

PAULA ROLLO

CHAPTER FOUR
Stealing The Baby Years

Where did my baby go?

It is truly amazing all the worries and fears we can come up with to dwell on with a new baby on the way. One huge concern for a lot of moms (and judgmental strangers) is the thought that having another child is some how robbing the first baby of something.

Whether it's the fear that you won't be able to spend adequate time with your first baby or worrying that you are taking his "baby years" from him and forcing him to grow up too quickly, these are very real concerns for a lot of people, myself included.

My son was not quite 13 months old when we found out we were expecting his sister. He was very much still my baby, and I struggled with thoughts of being able to care for two. I worried about sharing my love between multiple little ones. I didn't want to steal his baby-ness from him, and I certainly didn't want to deprive him of anything.

People are quick to put worries like these in our minds. Even the smallest of offhand comments have been known to keep many a pregnant woman up all night worrying! Not that I have experience with that at all…because I definitely never stayed up for hours at night worrying about everything that I couldn't control, including my capability to love more than one child. (You totally believe that right?)

I had wanted my kids to be close in age (mainly because I wanted to put pregnancies and diapers behind me ASAP), but that didn't stop the worries from overwhelming me after I became pregnant with our second.

I was stressed about all these things for a while, and then it dawned on me that if it was somehow "unfair" to an older child to have a sibling within a certain period of time, then it would also be "unfair" to be born a twin, or triplet. No one sees twins as being unfair to one another, and yet we fret day and night about the "perfect" timing between kiddos.

There is no magic formula for the best time. If you are pregnant with another kiddo, then this is a great time, because you will find a way to make it great.

This is a great time to have another baby, because you will find a way to make it great.

Figuring it out along the way is half the fun (…and half the stress, but whatevs!).

There are going to be difficulties in the transition no matter if the older child is 9 months old when his sibling is born or 17 years old. It's always a transition, and transitions are always a challenge.

That's the nature of change: it's uncomfortable.

You are not stealing anything from your older child. In fact, you are giving him a gift: the gift of a sibling, including the joy of being an older sibling and learning to love and be loved in fresh and amazing ways.

*You are not stealing anything from your older child. In fact, you are giving him a **gift**: the gift of a sibling.*

He may not be able to understand or appreciate that today, but 11 years from now when he views his little sibling as his best friend and closest confidant, I doubt he'll be complaining to you that you "stole" his baby years from him

It's Not Baby's Fault

I can't claim this sage wisdom as my own, as it was passed along to be by multiple different mothers further along in the motherhood journey than myself. When I asked other moms for advice about bringing home a second baby, this is something that came up a majority of the time. Don't blame the baby!

Until they brought it up, I hadn't even noticed how often I blamed things on the baby without even realizing what was doing . I certainly never thought about how it would affect my son's perception of his sister before she was even born.

"I can't run with you right now because the baby is making me tired."
"Mama's feeling sick right now because of the baby."
"I can't hold you right now because you are too heavy with the baby."
And so on.

A hundred times a day, both during pregnancy and afterwards, we have the opportunity to blame multiple negative things on the baby. It's true that many of the things I listed are genuinely happening as a direct result of the pregnancy, but it can start to make the older kiddo already think of the new baby in a negative light.

He could begin thinking "Mommy doesn't play with me as much because of the new baby" or "Mommy is tired and sick a lot because of the baby." An older child might be able to differentiate between the pregnancy causing it and the baby vindictively trying to steal mommy away, but a young toddler's brain can't necessarily comprehend that.

After receiving advice from many mommy-friends of mine, I started changing the way I phrased things. It was a very subtle change, but I just left the baby out of anything negative that I said to my toddler.

If I wasn't feeling up to running around with him, I would say just that. Rather than saying that it was because of baby or pregnancy, I would simply state "Mommy is feeling too tired to run right now," and possibly suggest a quieter activity that we could do together, like I mentioned in chapter one.

Instead of saying I was feeling sick because of the baby, I would just tell him that I was feeling sick. A toddler doesn't know the difference between illnesses anyway, so just stating that I was feeling sick was enough of an explanation for him.

By making this subtle change, I was able to talk about the baby in a positive and fun way instead of teaching him to think of her in a negative way before he even met her!

My son was only 21 months old when his sister was born, so I have no way of knowing what was going through his mind when he met her. He seemed excited that she had eyes and fingers like he did, but then he swiftly turned his attention to the cookies someone had brought to the hospital and was done with her for that time.

I don't know what he thought about on the drive home or if he even had an inkling about how much his life was about to change. I like to imagine that he had only good thoughts of his sister instead of a lot of worries and fears that I had unintentionally programmed into him.

It's such a small thing, but sometimes those small things end up being the biggest in the mind of a toddler.

Officially a Big Kid?

Speaking of new roles… In my experience, toddlers can have mixed feelings about suddenly being promoted to "big kid" status. While on the one hand little ones seem to jump at the chance to be referred to as "big" under any context, it can be a bit disconcerting too.

I remember specific times when my son would look at me with big questioning eyes and ask in his own way if he was still my baby. He wasn't quite old enough to get all the words in the right places, but if I could guess what his little heart was asking in that moment, I'd say that he wanted to know if he'd been replaced, if there was still the same amount of love in my heart for him, that there was before the new baby came along.

I remember cuddling him in my arms and assuring him that he will always be my baby. In fact, I made a habit of me wrapping him in a towel after bath and singing a special "baby" song. He loved being reminded that he was *still* my baby, even though there was a new little one in the house.

Occasionally, other people would try to tease that he was a big kid now, and no longer the baby, but I was always quick to reassure him that this was not the case. Each of my children will forever and always be my babies. Even when they grow up and move out, they will still hold the precious "baby" status that no one else in my life can claim.

I never take that title from them, unless they ask for it to be retired for a season, but that has yet to happen in our house. Yes, as they get older I may expect them to act like big kids and behave, but reassuring my "big boy" that he'll always be my baby doesn't cause regression in behavior. If anything, it lessens the difficulties he has because he knows that nothing has changed in my heart towards him, and that comforts him more than he has the ability to express.

My son loves the freedom that he has to be a "big

boy" and my baby interchangeably. One day he prefers one title and the next day, he may want to be called another, but I just try to roll with whichever term of endearment he prefers. Having a new baby doesn't change the status of my love for him, and if calling him "baby" now and then helps to assure him of this, I don't have a problem saying he's still my baby.

Little Chatterbox

If your little one is able to talk already, chances are they don't stop! My son rarely comes up for air when he gets going on a good story that he wants to share! This makes talking another great way to promote the sibling-bond before the baby arrives!

They say that babies can hear when you are about 16 weeks pregnant, which means every one can start talking to baby!

Asking your older child to sing to the baby in the belly or tell stories to the bump can be a fun way to help them start to get used to the idea of each other. The baby can learn her big sibling's voice, and it just might help your older child to realize that, yes, there is a baby in mama's tummy (my son kept forgetting).

You can also use that creativity that little ones possess to help you brainstorm baby names. Sure, you may get some strange ones like "purple-fairy-princess" or "zunkakid," but you never know if your little one might come up with the *perfect* baby name!

You could even settle on a few favorites and let the big sibling choose from them. Involving them in every process possible can make them feel so important!

My little guy was a bit too young to understand the whole naming process just yet, but if we ever have another, I'm hoping to involve him a bit more, even if it's just to hear all the fun little names he would come up with!

PAULA ROLLO

CHAPTER FIVE
Tools to Help Them Adjust

Books, bears, and practicing!

It's no surprise that having a new baby is a big adjustment, every time. It can take kids an extra long time to get used to the idea, simply because they have no point of reference for what is about to happen. Most especially if this is the first new sibling to come on the scene, kiddos really don't know what to expect.

We did several special things to help prepare our little guy ahead of time and try to give him a good idea about the transitions that were about to take place in our family. We did our best to keep it fun and positive, while also being realistic about the differences in our day-to-day life that would start taking place after Sister was born.

Since my husband and I both love to read, and our son loves storybooks, it seemed natural to start the adjusting and equipping process with books!

Books for the Big Kid

There are a lot of children's books on the market right now to help with the new baby transition. My son loves a good storybook, so we bought several of them to see what he identified with the most (and because I'm a paranoid control freak who didn't want to miss out on the perfect book that would single-handedly make our transition the easiest thing in the universe).

I do think that books can play a huge role in preparing a big sibling for their new role. Most kids love hearing stories, and picture books can explain things in more detail than would ever be possible in a regular conversation with a young child.

Of all the books we purchased and borrowed, it really came down to two that we absolutely loved. Each of these books talked about the new baby in a positive way and not as a challenge that needed to be overcome.

I love the way each book built excitement and understanding in my son's mind as we read them together. I highly recommend each of these to any family welcoming a new baby!

Hello Baby by Lizzy Rockwell – This book goes through the entire process, from pregnancy to bringing baby home. It's written from the perspective of the big brother, and he describes the doctor visits, feeling baby move in mama's belly, and even the noises baby makes when she comes home!

It's an adorable book that has really awesome images. There is one page that shows the cartoon mama in her underwear (it sounds weird, but it's really not). It depicts her big pregnant belly, and you can see through the belly to the baby inside. It talks about how the baby is growing inside there, how the baby eats, and that it's swimming in some water in mama's tummy.

This image really helped it "click" in my toddler's brain that there was, in fact, a baby in my belly. Prior to reading this book, he would always look at me like I was a lunatic when I tried to explain such an abstract concept, so I'm very thankful for the images that it helped him understand.

The book also talks about when mommy goes to the hospital to have the baby, and the boy's grandmother stays with him for a few days. It's very positive and talks about all the fun things that the little boy gets to do while they wait for time to visit mama & baby sister in the hospital. I loved the way it built excitement and anticipation for that time, instead of making it sound scary or depicting it in such a way that it would feel like mommy was abandoning him. My son would always ask questions after this section to clarify that he and his grandma would get to do all those fun things, too.

All in all, this was a fantastic transition book, and I highly recommend it!

I'm a Big Brother/I'm a Big Sister by Joanna Cole – This book is more for after the baby comes home. We bought this book ahead of time and then gave it to our son in the hospital after he met his baby sister. It was one of his "big brother" gifts (see chapter 6), and it quickly became a favorite.

Once again, the book is from the perspective of the older child, who explains all about the new baby coming home. The older child compares himself to the new baby. They talk about things that baby does and how to take care of baby.

It also discusses ways that baby and big sibling are different. There are things that the big sibling can do that baby can't yet and so forth. At the very end, the child goes into detail about how he can do special things because he's big, and at the very end he says: "I'm special in a new way, too," and then talks about how special it is to be a big sibling!

I thought it was very well done, particularly in the way they address that mommy and daddy love the new baby and that mommy and daddy definitely love big brother/big sister.

We borrowed a number of books from the library and purchased even more from consignment stores, but The two mentioned above were by far the stand outs. We happened upon a little golden book entitled *The*

New Baby and really enjoyed the story (with all it's vintage photos and details) but it is no longer in print. The only other book we actually purchased was:

Arthur and the Baby by Marc Brown - I felt like this book might have been more appropriate for an older preschooler, not a toddler. The book mentions and addresses several worries that an older child might have concerning a new baby, which could be helpful if he or she has heard things from friends or has thought up some of these things, but I personally skipped a few pages of the book here and there, because I didn't want to add any concerns to my son's mind that he hadn't already thought about on his own.

Overall, books were one of our very favorite ways of preparing our little guy to be a big sibling. It was really the only way that he could see and understand the transition that was about to take place. He was the first of his friends to become a big sibling, so he hadn't even seen it play out in real life in someone else's home. Seeing the children in the story books becoming siblings, welcoming a new baby into their home *forever* was a really fun way to introduce the concept to him.

But we didn't stop there with our pre-baby preparations!

The Baby Doll: *They're Not Just For Girls*

When my son was about 18 months old, I bought him a baby doll. This earned us a lot of strange looks.

My husband even said: "you want to buy him WHAT? Why???" when I first told him of my plan. But looking back, I am so glad that I bought it for him.

You see, as a young toddler, my little guy hadn't been around babies much. Let's face it, he wasn't even around things that he needed to be all that gentle with. His toys are all made from seemingly indestructible plastic, and we always remove all breakables from a room before he enters it. Words like "soft" and "gentle" just weren't in his vocabulary at 18 months. As I was thinking about this one day, I decided he needed some practice. Hence the baby doll.

We bought the cheapest one we could find and began our "gentle" routine. We'd rock baby, pat her gently, and work on the difference between patting and hitting, which is a surprisingly difficult concept for an 18 month old to grasp.

He was a little guy, so he needed lots of repetition, but a baby doll was the perfect avenue to provide that practice and teach those new concepts in a way that was safe and fun!

If you have a little girl, you may already have been practicing these things with her baby dolls for a long time, and you could just use this stage to reinforce what she already knows about being sweet with babies. But for some kiddos, this can be an entirely new concept.

I know that some people still might think it's a little strange to buy a baby doll for a little boy, but I actually think it's quite healthy. Training boys to be good daddies can start at a very young age. Teaching them to interact with smaller children and even care for them is such a beautiful skill, both for this stage of life and for their adulthood.

Little boys can (and should, in my opinion) play daddy just like little girls play mommy! No one tells my husband he's lame for caring for his family and loving on his kids. In fact, I love and respect him so much more because of the way he cares for our kids and plays with them every chance he gets.

There is nothing wrong with teaching boys that it's wonderful to be a good daddy. It's a great skill that can be taught early on, with even the smallest of kids!

There is nothing wrong with teaching boys that it's wonderful to be a good daddy.

We bought our doll 5 months before the baby was due. I think that was a good amount of time to start transitioning and learning the new 'gentle' concept. We kept baby up out of reach when we were not playing with it so that it didn't accidentally get stepped on or thrown about during regular playtime, thus undoing all the teaching activities that we had been working on!

If your little one is like mine, some days he might not be interested in playing with baby at all, and that's okay! Just have it there to teach the words when he is interested and don't worry about it when he's not. This should be a fun exercise in learning new words and concepts for the little one, and you definitely want your child to associate babies with fun, not dread getting into trouble for playing incorrectly.

The Feeding Nook

Another thing that can be addressed before baby arrives is how often the baby will be eating. Feeding time is such a difficult transition because it's one of the main times of day that you cannot immediately cater to the needs of your older child the way that he might be used to.

In order to make this a smooth transition and curb any jealousy before it can begin, I suggest making a little feeding nook. It doesn't have to be anything fancy, but it can do a lot to build confidence in the older kiddo.

Add a mini rocker next to the big one, or even a little stool so that your older child has a special space near you to sit during feeding time. I can't tell you how many times my son would try to climb in my lap (or push his sister OUT of my lap!) when I was nursing the baby. I really wish I would have made a nook *before* she arrived and set the precedent of him sitting next to me during that time.

Once you've set up the chairs, bring a basket of books over, or a doll bed, (so the doll can eat when baby eats!) so that there are plenty of fun things to do in the nook.

Chances are, most of the time the older kiddo will elect to play something else while you feed the baby, but having the option there will let the older child know that they aren't being forgotten or ignored, and it will make them feel welcome. This does wonders for the behavior of the older kiddo, believe me!

Sleepovers

One of the very last things we did to prepare before the baby was born was practicing sleepovers. I'm a stay at home mom, and our son had never been to daycare, so the thought of leaving him for a few days while I was in the hospital was a bit concerning!

We decided to do a couple of practice runs leading up to my due date, letting him stay the night with my in laws here and there. He took it like a champ and loved every minute of it, while I was a bundle of stress (shocking, right?).

I actually learned a lot during his little sleepover. I thought it was just one more way I was preparing him, letting him experience being away from me in a fun way, before he *had* to be away from me while I was in the hospital, but really I learned much more from it than he did!

There's something about letting go, watching your little one do something that you don't feel ready for them to do just yet, and realizing that they can do it. I could see just how big he was getting and how, even though I still viewed him as this little tiny infant, he was growing into a little boy able to survive in loving environments without me there every last second.

As stressful as it was, it was also comforting to me, knowing that he was happy as he could possibly be with my in-laws. It was just one less thing to worry about when baby decided to make her debut. I knew that he would do great with the overnights without mommy or daddy.

I say the sleepovers are for preparing the kiddo, but maybe they are more for preparing the mama. I guess it just depends on how your family works. My son has never been the clingy type, though, so it was natural for him to do over nights with grandma without batting an eye. It served to show me that my baby was growing up and ready for his new job as "big brother" in our family.

CHAPTER SIX
Settling into Siblinghood

New family dynamics when baby comes home

Honestly, it's going to take a little bit of time for things to settle down into the new normal that comes with the new family member, but the transition doesn't have to be crazy. You've done so much to prepare your little one, and now you just have to help them through the transition in to your new lives together with your growing family.

One of the best places to start this process is in the hospital. Think through how you want to introduce the siblings to one another. Some parents choose to let their little ones be present during the birth, while others wait until later on to bring the older kids in to meet the baby and see mama after every one has been cleaned up. It's a unique situation and a decision that will probably be different for every family.

For us, we chose not to have our son present for her birth, but to bring him in after everything had calmed down. This ended up working best, especially since baby girl decided to arrive just after his bedtime (he goes to bed at 7 pm).

I knew that I was in labor when I was putting him to sleep and ended up having to rush out of his room because my contractions were coming so fast. I didn't want him to be concerned about the faces and grimaces I was making!

Sister was born around 8:30pm (yes, I do have ridiculously fast labors, but that's a story for another time). My mother-in-law brought my son up to meet his new sister around lunchtime the next day. This gave everyone time to rest (and me time to shower) before they were introduced.

He came into the hospital room looking like a giant of child, certainly much bigger than I remembered him being the night before. Something about holding his 7 pound sister all night made me realize just how much he had grown in the past year.

He crawled up on the bed with me and took a peek in the blanket at his sister. "Baby!" he exclaimed, and then began pointing out her body parts and comparing, "Baby nose, me nose…baby ears, me ears," and so on. It was really cute to see him connecting with her for those 45 seconds before he got bored and began exploring the hospital room.

Maybe it was his age, or maybe it's just because of the

feisty little boy that he is, but he didn't spend too much time up on the bed having a magical moment with me and his new baby sister. But I was okay with that. They met, and he got to move on to more interesting things, like trying to poke all of the buttons on my hospital bed and exploring the snacks that various people had brought by my room before he arrived.

It was really cute to see him connecting with her for those 45 seconds before he got bored and began exploring the hospital room.

After the not-quite-full minute of had passed, I decided to bring out the gifts!

To Gift or Not to Gift

A popular trend right now is gifts for the new big sibling on the day that the baby is born. Some choose to have the gifts be "from" the new baby to the big sibling and make it a small gift exchange.

Oftentimes, the new sibling gives the new baby a small toy, as well. Some parents avoid the gifts all together. And then other parents give presents exclusively to the new big sibling, letting them know that they are special presents from mommy and daddy to congratulate them for becoming a big brother or sister.

I don't think there is any right or wrong way to do this, but it's worth thinking about what would be the best option for your family.

We decided to make a box of presents for our little guy because we wanted the day his sister was born to be epically awesome for his little one-year-old self. The main way to make something epic at that age is to provide presents, so that's what we did.

Here's a funny side note: To this day, the thing our son remembers about the day he met his sister was not the presents I had oh-so-carefully selected and prepared for him, and it certainly was not meeting his sister for the first time.

It was the chocolate chip cookies that my sister brought me to munch after labor. Yep, the cookies. If you corner him today and ask about the time he went to the hospital to meet sis, his eyes will glaze over and he will start describing the cookies that he got to eat. It's the little things, people, the little things.

But back to the great gift debate: It really all comes down to what you think your child would respond to best. Maybe forgoing presents would teach a good lesson that the world is not going to entirely revolve around the older child now, or maybe exchanging gifts will create a special memory in the older child's mind, forging an immediate sibling bond that will last forever.

Perhaps you can prepare a special box of presents that will remind your older child that he is still loved and remembered, even though mommy and daddy are in the hospital with the new baby for a few days. Only you know what will work best for your family, and truthfully, there are more important things than whether or not you provide the perfect big sibling gift at the ideal moment. Trust your instincts, and go with what you think would be best for your kiddo.

What to Give

So if you are like me, you might have decided to create a gift box of epic goodies for your older child to receive on the day of his sibling's birth.

In hindsight, I should have included the cookies in this box, so you may want to consider adding those to yours. I'm pretty sure my son's primary love language is "cookies," so I'm not sure why I didn't think of it myself, but there you have it.

Some parents select new toys for the older child to play with in the hospital, like a new dump truck, a doll, or a special coloring book. Finding a special toy that your child will cherish for a long time is always a difficult task with the unpredictability of kiddos, but it can be fun, too!

When I was choosing gifts, I decided to go for things that held specific meaning for the stage of life that we were in at the moment (you see that control freak planner coming out in me again don't you?).

I included the big brother book that I mentioned earlier, and a Build-A-Bear. Now before you roll your eyes and tell me your kid doesn't need *another* stuffed animal (trust me, mine doesn't either!) hear me out on the bear.

This was actually one of the very best things we did for our little man, and he still snuggles that little animal! Obviously, at Build-A-Bear you get to build stuffed animals, but they also have a feature that allows you to add a recording to the bears. I think this costs around $8 extra, and since I bought the cheapest little animal they had, my total came out under $20, since I didn't buy any of the cutesy little outfits.

In the store, I made a recording of myself saying "I love you" to him, and they stuffed it into the paw of his new animal.

My little boy and I hadn't been separated much at all before his sister was born, and he'd spent the night without me only once before, so I thought it might help him to have my voice with him at night as he was falling asleep and even throughout the day if he started to miss me.

Since I don't work outside the home, he is used to having me by his side *at all times,* so this really helped him know that I loved him, even from afar!

I gave him his Build-A-Bear (dog) in the hospital right before he left for home with my mother-in-law. She texted me later and told me that he pushed the button to listen to me saying "I love you" to him for over an hour straight in the car and as they ran errands. She said she could hear him pushing it in bed as he fell asleep later that night, as well.

I think the bear helped him tremendously, especially since he was so young that he couldn't really comprehend the birthing process or why mommy couldn't be home to tuck him in to bed.

Those were the two main things we got for our son's big brother gifts, but here are a couple more ideas.

Big Brother/ Big Sister Official Scrubs – We didn't do these, but I think they are absolutely adorable! You can order them on amazon for pretty cheap, and the big sibling can dress up just like a doctor! I have a friend whose son wore his scrubs to every doctor visit and whenever he would come see the baby in the hospital. He was so proud of himself to be in an "official" big brother outfit! Scrubs make for pretty adorable "first pictures," too!

A Photo Book – This can be another fun gift idea for an older sibling. You could even make it a fun project to work on together before baby comes, if you have an older child. You can create a scrapbook of photos of the older child's life thus far, including your pregnancy with him or her. Show off all the stages of her life, and be sure to include lots of tiny-baby pictures from when she was born. Then, leave some

73

pages in the back to fill in with new pictures of the baby and pictures of the new siblings together! Assigning the new big sibling as "official photographer" or "official scrapbooker" can make them feel very important and included in the entire process. My little guy was too small to do these things when his sister was born, but I always enjoy looking at the photo books that my friends have made with their older children. They always turn out super cute, and the kids feel so special to have a scrapbook all their own.

Really, the possibilities are endless when it comes to the types of presents you could give the big sibling, so I'll stop with these. It all depends on what you think he or she would respond best to, and what would help him or her feel special as they take on the new role of big sibling!

Coming Home

With everything that we did to prepare him, I'll still never forget the look on my son's face when he woke up from his nap to find me home from the hospital with his baby sister.

His chubby little toddler face just stared at her with such an adorable mix of emotion. So much was conveyed in that moment when he found her sleeping in her cradle in my room. Awe, concern, curiosity, and maybe just a hint of shock and jealousy.

Most of all, he was excited that mommy and daddy

were finally home from the hospital to play with him again. Since baby was sleeping, we were able to jump right in to the important business of playing with our little guy.

Bringing baby home wasn't the momentous occasion that I was expecting. It just felt natural to have her there with us and to start settling in to a family of four.

Of course, our little guy was curious and probably wondering how long she'd be staying, but he was truly a champ that first day home, happy to have his whole family together again, even if it included someone extra.

What if He Doesn't Like the Baby?

This is not something we dealt with specifically, but I've heard so many stories. It is certainly worth mentioning.

What if the older sibling doesn't like the baby, or asks when you'll be returning the baby to the hospital?

That might happen, and you know what? It's okay. There have been many a big sibling who was not the world's biggest fan of the new baby, requested to take it back to the hospital pronto, and/or cried when they realized baby was here to stay.

The awesome (and sometimes embarrassing) thing

about kids is that they speak their minds, even when we don't want to hear it. So don't worry if your little one isn't thrilled at the sight of your littlest one. Give them time. Change is hard on everybody, most particularly little ones who have not had very much opportunity to learn to adapt to new circumstances thus far in their lives.

Not being in love with the baby right away doesn't mean that the kids will never get along or that they will fight all the time as they get older. I can think of a few families right off the top of my head whose older siblings weren't overjoyed when the new baby came home, but the two kids ended up being best friends throughout their lives.

Kids are going to be honest and share exactly what they are feeling, even when it just might make mommy cry. That's totally okay. Roll with it and move on. Continue making baby's arrival something fun and positive for everyone in the family, and your little one will catch up as the change becomes normal and the fear of the unknown turns into excitement over having a new playmate!

The awesome thing about parenting (and life in general) is that it takes time. Everything doesn't have to be perfect right now. Just keep trying, keep working, keep loving, and keep praying!

Keep your cool and your calm, and eventually your

big kid will follow suit and realize that although things have changed, it's a good change and will mean lots of fun adventures in the future!

Section Three

Making the Transition

PAULA ROLLO

CHAPTER SEVEN
Sharing Attention

Balancing meal times, car trips and hugs

One thing I've learned about toddlers is that, often, their misbehavior is a cry for attention, whether they realize it or not. The first three months after sister was born were the roughest in our house and required me to be very intentional with how I was spending my time.

My husband had to go back to work shortly after Sister was born, so many of these transitions were left to me to figure out on my own. It wasn't the simplest thing in the world, but we learned a lot during that time period, and our whole family grew closer together despite the challenges!

To help my little boy out, I found that doing simple things to keep his routine on track did wonders for his behavior.

Before baby was born, I would always go into his room after he woke up and we'd have a few minutes of one-on-one playtime before he ventured out into the living room looking for breakfast.

After baby was born, I'd open the door to his room with a swift "good morning" as I rushed back down the hall to change Sister's diaper or finish nursing. I realized one morning what a huge change this was for him and that it could possibly be the cause of the uncanny number of tantrums we were experiencing every morning.

So I decided to experiment. The next day, I changed Sister, nursed her, and put her back to bed, all before I went and opened his door in the morning. He had to wait maybe an extra 10 minutes before he came out of his room, but we were able to have our one-on-one playtime first thing in the morning just like before his sister was born.

The change in his behavior that morning was *astonishing*. He was so happy and carefree after we played. He wasn't unkind to his sister, and the tantrums were much fewer in number. It was amazing. I did things this way for the rest of the week and enjoyed much happier mornings with my son.

Sometime in the second week, I forgot my plan and rushed in to get him up in the middle of nursing, and what do you know? It was a crazy morning once again. I realized my mistake halfway through the morning, when he was in the middle of his 5000th tantrum and I was about to lose my cool not for the first time that morning.

Instead of reacting, I stopped everything, put the baby in her swing and led him to his room. And we played. Just he and I. Sister fussed a bit, and I let her fuss, showing him now that he is just as important to me as his sister, reassuring him that I will be there when he needs me, just like I'm there when she does.

It was a good lesson for both of us and one I haven't forgotten. My son is still my baby, and he still needs me. He may not literally require my milk and he can get to sleep without me rocking him, but that doesn't mean he doesn't need one-on-one mommy time. or reassurance that I'll always have his back, and I'll be there for the important task of Tonka truck driver or tickle-MOMster.

Attention means the world to toddlers. My advice would be to mentally schedule times in your day for one-on-one playtime with your older child. This might be during the baby's naptime or during her happiest time of day when she would be content in the rocker for a few minutes. Just 15 minutes twice a day could make all the difference in his feeling loved and *your feeling sane.*

If you find your toddler acting totally out of character, think about when you played *just* with him last, and if it's been awhile, try to make it happen as soon as you can. Even if it's just for a few moments, take the time to show him that you care through play.

I'm learning that the largest way that I can show my kids that I care about them is to do what they love most: play. Even when I'm tired. And even when the baby needs me. Sometimes we just need to play.

I also played with Brother while the baby was in my lap sometimes, slowly incorporating her into our everyday lives. He enjoyed showing her his toys and driving cars up and down her belly.

Those were special times as well, as he slowly came to accept her as a new member of our family. I didn't shove her aside every time my son wanted some attention, but there were definitely times when it was evident that he needed a tangible way to measure our love, and during those times, I'd do my best to drop what I could and play.

Regression: *Not Again!*

When baby comes, it is completely normal for the older child to regress back into some old (less than pleasant) behaviors. Some potty-trained toddlers stop using the toilet. Kiddos who may have passed the tantrum stage months ago may find themselves throwing tantrums with the best of them once again. Though the behavior may vary, some type of regression is to be expected.

Let me just tell you, I am *so* glad that someone warned me about this. You see, Brother hit an insanely rough tantrum patch when I was around 6 or 7 months pregnant with Sister. I do not look back on those days with even the slightest bit of nostalgia. It was just plain rough and I was *overjoyed* when it was over.

When he started throwing tantrums *again* a couple weeks after Sister was born, I was really bummed and dreading the idea of dealing with months of tantrums again. As much as I didn't want it to happen, I was pretty sure that it would happen, and I was right! So when the wailing and the screaming started up again, I was ready to be consistent, and it didn't completely knock me off my feet. *I knew something was coming.*

I'm not trying to scare you or make you worry that your toddler is going to turn into some crazy urchin the moment your new baby is born. Thankfully, that's not how it happens. Just know that it might be a little rocky as big brother or big sister figures out their place in the family again, but it's totally do-able.

The nice thing about regression (yes, I did say nice thing…) is that you've already faced the behavior once. Although you might not be too keen on dealing with it a second time, you do have an idea of how to work through and correct whatever behavior your little one regresses to.

It might be challenging, and it's certainly less-than-ideal, but you can do it! I was surprised that dealing with tantrums the second time wasn't quite the emotional and mental struggle for me that it was the first time. My perspective was better, and I knew that we wouldn't be dealing with them forever. We had already overcome them once, so I knew we could do it again!

Whether your little one struggles with regression in whining, tantrums, potty training or something completely different, you've already gotten through it once, and you can totally handle it again!

Who is This Child?

When baby girl was about two weeks old, we hit a particular low point in our transition process. I'm not sure if it had just finally settled into my son's mind that *"this baby is here to stay"* or what, but suddenly nothing was working anymore and my poor son was having a rough time.

Of course by, "my poor son was having a rough time," I really mean that we were ALL having a rough time. And going a bit crazy. The tantrums seemed to be endless again and I could just tell that he was constantly on the edge of a meltdown (as was I).

All my cute little tactics weren't helping, so I decided to do something a bit more drastic and call a babysitter. For my daughter.

Leaving my two-week old for any period of time seemed partially insane to my still-hormonal self, but I thought it might be the best thing for my son, and let's be honest, the baby was going to sleep the entire time anyway.

We hopped in the car and drove the 10 minutes to my friend's house. I nursed the baby, and then my little boy and I drove back home to play. We had a good two hours of one on one playtime, without any worry of needing to go turn on the baby's swing or return her pacifier to her.

Since I was exclusively breastfeeding, we had to go pick her up rather quickly, but those two hours made an entire world of difference to my son.

I only did this one time, but it was all he really needed. Some extra assurance that I was still there, that I was still *his* mama. In fact, about an hour into our playtime he began asking me "where Sissa?" and was a bit concerned about why she was not at home. This was the first time that he showed signs of recognizing that she belonged with us, not anywhere else.

Way to warm your mama's heart after a long week, kiddo! With our emotions doing much better, we were ready to conquer the world together… or maybe just figure out how the daily logistics of having two kids and only one mama works out.

Sure, Daddy is around to help on weekends, and for a bit of time before bed every night, but the bulk of the day is still all on mama. I needed to figure this out.

Who Goes First? Finding That Balance

One of my biggest worries about having baby #2 was figuring out my days logistically. Who do I get out of the car first? If both kids are screaming, who do I help first? Who eats when, and how do I handle multiple bedtimes? Who gets the first hug and kiss after falling?

It seems like such a logistical nightmare, and truly, sometimes it is. There will be times when both kids will be screaming. There will most certainly be times that all your kiddos feel that they will waste away into nothingness if they don't eat at this exact moment in time. Such is life with more than one child vying for the "center-of-the-known-universe" spot in your family.

While all of those things may seem incredibly intimidating right now, they are just facts of life. It's been my experience that the second kiddo learns patience a lot sooner than the first kiddo did. Poor sister had to wait to be nursed, or wait to be put to bed *far* more than her big brother ever had to wait. When he was born, my entire world revolved around him, but now that I've got two little ones in my orbit, my time has to be balanced a bit more between them. They are both learning at a young age that the entire universe will not take a pause at their every whim, and really, that's not a bad lesson to learn.

Logistically, you will quickly learn what works best for your family, and you will probably have to re-adjust multiple times as things change and babies grow. I found that I was constantly re-adapting to life and how to time everything as naptimes changed, bedtimes got later, eating habits were switched around, and car seats were outgrown!

For example: While the baby was in a baby carrier
type of car seat, I'd put her seat on the ground next to
me while I got Brother in the car first (making sure
the baby seat is in a safe spot where cars won't hit it
of course). When getting *out* of the car, I'd do the
opposite, baby would get out first (in the carrier
again), and she'd wait on the ground while I got her
brother out.

When she moved out of the carrier into a "big girl
seat," I switched it up. I would carry her to her seat
first and get her buckled in while Brother (still just 2
years old and not to be trusted not to run into traffic)
stood in the door with me, my body blocking him
from the parking lot traffic. After Sis is all buckled in,
I'd take Brother to his side and get him all secured.
Getting them out of the car, she goes first again and I
hold her while I undo his buckles and he can climb
out of his seat himself.

Confused yet? Don't worry, you will find your
groove! It *can* be done, and you can do it!!!
As far as simultaneous meltdowns go, you just have
to wing it. Generally, the kid that's screaming the
loudest gets help first, but sometimes I break this rule
if one kid's need will be a much faster fix than the
other kiddo. When this happens I do the fast one
first, so he (or she) doesn't have to suffer through a
long wait while I'm helping the other one.

I might throw together a quick snack for Brother
before I nurse Sis, because it will take me 20 minutes
to nurse her, compared with whipping up a sandwich
in two minutes. The baby can cry for the two minutes

it takes for me to make the boy a sandwich so he doesn't have to wait.

As crazy as it may seem right now, you will find your groove. Things that seem wild and intimidating now will soon be a simple part of your every day life. You figured it all out once with your first baby, you can definitely do it again. Yes, it will be hard, but that doesn't mean you can't handle it, because you can. Pregnancy is hard, parenting is hard, being a woman is hard, and yet you succeed at these things every day. If today was a chaotic mess, don't worry about it! Just keep going and realize that tomorrow just might be pure chaos too. That's totally okay! Chaos is not a sign of failure; it's a sign of children. Just roll with it and try to find the laughter in the midst of the turmoil.

Chaos is not a sign of failure; it's a sign of children.

These seasons really do go by quickly, to be replaced by all sorts of other fun and challenging times of parenthood. We're on a wild ride, my friends, but it's a fun one!

CHAPTER EIGHT
Being Consistent

"We don't hit baby," & other things that should be obvious.

Regression is tough, so how should we handle it? I'm not going to tell you how to discipline your child. I can't pretend to know what the best ways of correction and teaching are for your precious ones, but I do know one thing is true across the board: Consistency is key.

I went into my first week with both babies by myself, knowing that I would need to work hard and start out being consistent. Kids learn fast, and I knew if I even let my guard down for a few days, I would have to work twice as hard to reinforce the rules that I'd been teaching him for months.

Being consistent meant jumping up in the middle of nursing to correct naughty behavior. It meant taking hold of teachable moments, even when I felt exhausted and would have rather just let something slide. It sometimes meant taking a moment to enforce a rule with my son before I changed the baby's diaper or swaddled her up for bedtime.

It was definitely a rough first week or two, but I am so glad I mentally prepped myself for it and told myself to be consistent. I truly believe that those weeks set the foundation for the rest of our transitional period. After testing me *on everything* for a solid week, he started to settle down. He figured out that he didn't have free reign over our home just because I was nursing his sister.

He quickly learned that I would still enforce our rules even if it meant inconveniencing myself or stopping in the middle of a diaper change. There is definitely a fine line between giving positive attention for the naughty behavior (and thereby teaching the kiddo that he just needs to act up to snatch your attention away from baby) and teaching consistency.

Only you can find that perfect balance with your precious kiddos! Keep trying and prepare yourself to be consistent.

If you are going to have help the first few weeks at home (I envy you, since I never really did!), make sure you have a talk with whoever will be helping out and explain your plan of action for enforcing rules and curbing naughty behavior.

It can be easy to feel like you need to give the kiddo a pass because they are going through a hard transition, but truly, the more you can keep life the same for them, the better it will be for all of you.

In my opinion, this includes keeping the rules that they know in place and enforcing them in the way they would expect. It will help them feel secure, knowing that this small part of their life hasn't been turned on its head, even if it's something as insignificant as the house rules and discipline tactics.

Be Prepared

In order to be consistent, you have to be prepared. You know your kiddo better than anyone else, so if you take some time to think through his behavior on his good AND bad days, you can probably come up with some pretty good ideas about how he might (mis)behave when he's having an off day after baby comes.

Knowing what to expect goes a long way in saving a mama's sanity! We know that regression is normal, but that doesn't make it *easy* necessarily, does it? (I wish!)

It really just comes down to using the tools that you have at your disposal to carry you through the transition stage.

Remember those closet toys and strategic restful play that we talked about back in chapter one? Those come in handy again after baby is born! Kiddo having a rough morning? Pull out some special toys from the closet and distract him with something "new" to play with.

One thing my son LOVED to do was make as much noise as physically possible while the baby was sleeping. As frustrating as this was, I knew I just needed to be better prepared for those times, so I decided to start planning little quiet activities for him. My guy loves to paint, so we'd get out the finger paints and let him have his quiet play-time while baby slept.

Baby's nap time(s) are also a great time to pull out toys with small pieces that baby can't have. Things like little board games, or small building blocks can make quiet times special times.

I know several moms who create busy bags for their older kids to have after a new baby was born. These are perfect because they are small andsimple, but they really keep the kids busy!

My son loves the busy bags that we've made for him. Each one can hold his attention for a surprisingly lengthy amount of time!

The point is, you know your kiddo, and can probably guess most of the challenges you will face with your older child. Take some time to think about it and prepare yourself, brainstorm ideas with your husband to find clever ways to avoid meltdowns and keep all the kiddos (and by extension, adults) in a good mood!

But even with all the preparation, there will be some surprises. There were countless things that I had to say in the first few weeks of my daughter's life that I never would have imagined! Just simple "common sense" stuff that is obvious to every one who is not a toddler.

We Don't Hit Baby: *Tips for Redirection*

"We don't hit baby…or pull her hair, or drag her around the house by her arm, or scream in her face, or cover her head with a blanket or…."

The list goes on and on. Things I never would have imagined even needing to address, they all need to be addressed after baby comes home.

I never thought I'd have to make a specific rule about NOT "sharing" toys with baby's face. Or specify that "big patting" is the same as hitting and also not okay. But alas, such rules had to be made, and the obvious had to be pointed out to my boy more often that I ever would have dreamed.

It's hard, because a toddler is so curious about the new little one. He wants to test his boundaries and figure out how he can interact with this tiny little creature. His curiosity can lead to a lot of bad ideas and even more good intentions turned wrong.
It got to the point where I started to feel bad because I needed to tell my son "no!" about something regarding the baby. All. The. Time.

I didn't want him to start associating her with getting in trouble, but obviously I couldn't just ignore the fact that he was trying to sit on her lap and then "patting" the soft spot on her head in typically rough toddler fashion.

I found that redirection worked best in these situations. Instead of saying "NO-DON'T-DO-THAT-STOP-RIGHT-NOW" like I wanted to, I would try to act very excited while directing him to her feet. "Hey buddy, she really likes it when you tickle her feet, so can you try that now?"

After working with him on tickling and making it a fun experience, I would address why it is a bad idea to try to sit on a newborn or share a Tonka truck with her face.

Sure, there were times when he was deliberately mean to her to try to get my attention, but it's usually pretty obvious when a child is doing it for attention and when they are truly just trying to figure out what to do with the new baby.

Redirecting to something they *can* do with baby seemed to work best for our little guy, and I've heard the same from a lot of other more seasoned mamas as well. Make it fun, but still set clear boundaries about the proper way to interact with the new baby.

Too. Much. Help.

There is a miniscule line between a toddler's help and their chaos. In fact, sometimes I don't think there is even a line at all. It's all the same. Big siblings love to be helpers. They love to feel like they are taking care of the new baby and participating in the duties of nurturing the new little one.

My son became an expert at shoving his sister's pacifier into her mouth, *most especially after she was already sleeping soundly*. He was also an impeccable sharer, mainly of objects that were too heavy for her tiny body, and like I said earlier, he usually felt that he needed to share said objects with his sister's face.

> *My son became an expert at shoving his sister's pacifier into her mouth, most especially after she was already sleeping soundly.*

Oh, the help of a toddler that really causes 10,000 times as many problems as it solves!

This was one of my biggest transitional struggles, because I didn't want to crush his little spirit. The boy clearly wanted to be involved in his sister's life, but goodness he just WOKE UP THE SLEEPING BABY!

At times, I just wanted to cry as I rocked the screaming baby to sleep for the second or third time, or dashed across the room to save her precious button nose from the business end of a toy screwdriver. Toddlers epitomize chaos, and it somehow seems to increase as you add a new baby to the mix. Prepare yourself now for lots and lots of "help" from the big kid.

Prepare yourself for lots of "help" from the big kid.

I eventually wised up and started to keep in mind an arsenal helping tasks for him. When I saw him heading for the sleeping babe, I would excitedly ask for help from a "big boy" to either quietly sing to the baby, fold her diapers, or eat chocolate--really anything to get him away from her sleeping form and rescue my sanity.

I had plans and backup plans and would request his help with various things throughout the day. Eventually, the lure of helping wore off, as I would ask him to do things and he started denying me. But then, I also didn't have to worry about him sharing toys on her head (as much) any more, so it really evened out.

Redirecting the help is very similar to redirecting the interactions. It's all about making baby a positive thing in the older child's life and not a pinnacle of trouble and limitations.

Ways Big Siblings Can Help

There are so many good reasons to say 'no' to an older sibling, especially when it comes to interacting with the new baby. Which is why it can be so helpful to have a list of tasks that they can do, always in your mind. This can help you redirect the wrong type of help into something safe and fun. Here are a few of our favorites:

1. Tickling baby's feet
2. Singing a song for baby (Twinkle Twinkle Little Star is a favorite at our house)
3. Choosing baby's next outfit
4. Folding or stacking (clean) diapers
5. Patting baby's belly
6. Coloring a picture for baby's room
7. Making silly faces at baby
8. Making funny noises for baby
9. Turning on/off the baby swing
10. Fetching burp cloths
11. Drying baby bottles
12. "Reading" to baby
13. Finding pacifiers
14. Shaking a rattle for baby
15. When in a really tough spot, you can always redirect to a toy or another activity *away* from baby.

CONCLUSION
What's It Really Like?

I have an entire arsenal of stories that I could share with you about the season of life you are about to enter. There are crazy stories, like the time my son hit the sleeping baby in the head for no reason at all.

But for every wonky and terrifying thing like that, there are at least a hundred beautiful experiences that come in this stage of life as well.

There's the way my daughter now wakes up saying "Bubba? Bubba?" and pointing to his room as soon as I lift her from her bed.

There's the way the big brother takes his role so seriously and looks out for his baby sis on the playground, grabbing her hand and glaring at anyone who he thinks might be bothering her.

Watching them grow up together is an absolute joy. Sure, it's messy and they have their little fights as well, but at the end of the day watching them love each other is truly one of the greatest joys of my entire life. It makes every little bump along the road to transitioning to life together more than worth it.

Together

Having another baby is a lot of things. It's scary, intimidating daunting and worrisome. But it's also a wonderful new adventure filled with joy, love, fun and so much beautiful chaos.

Things will change, and you will all grow together as you learn new things about yourselves and each other. Pregnancy is usually harder the second time around, but that doesn't mean that everything will be. You've been doing this whole mommy-thing for a while now and you will continue to get better at it.

Baby #2 might not do everything the same way that your first did them, and you will have all sorts of new tricks to learn, but you can do it! If you figured out baby #1 than you can surely learn all the needs and cues of babies two, three, four and so on.

That's the thing about us mamas; we're always learning as we go. There's always something new that our babies are teaching us, and that's kinda the beauty of it. They keep us on our toes, keep us laughing, and keep us young.

Whatever may come in the next few months (and years), don't freak out too much.

You are an expert on your children. God chose you for them, and you can do this.

The days might not always be easy, but they can still be fun. The days will probably never be quiet, but that does not mean that they will be without peace. You've got this, mama. You've got this.

PAULA ROLLO

Confessions of an Imperfect Mother

Sneak Peek

Confessions of an Imperfect Mother is a series on my blog. I've selected a few of the most popular posts in the series and turned them into an ebook. You can get copy this free ebook by subscribing to my blog at www.BeautyThroughImperfection.com/subscribe This is a sneak peek at two of the chapters in the book.

I Can't Enjoy Every Minute
But I'm enjoying the journey.

As moms, we are frequently encouraged to "just enjoy it" or "love every minute" of our days. While I can appreciate the sentiment (I know they years pass by too fast), I still find the application to be somewhat impossible, which is why I have stopped trying to enjoy every minute of motherhood.

There are certain aspects of motherhood that I do not enjoy. No matter how hard I've tried, I still hate breastfeeding. I will never love changing diapers, and although I've learned to understand and tolerate tantrums, I will never enjoy enduring them.

Motherhood is hard. And with it comes all sorts of challenges, not all of which can be enjoyed. Attempting to love every moment leaves me feeling guilty and inadequate, because I just can't do it.

So I've abandoned that endeavor. I no longer try to enjoy every last second of motherhood.

I've started doing something else instead. Because even though I can't enjoy every minute, I know that I can find much more joy in my days than I am currently experiencing. I can be a much more joyful mama to my littles, and I can definitely enjoy my *days* more, even if I can't enjoy every *minute*.

I'm learning to find joy in every day. To search for something beautiful throughout my day, something lovely in my children (even when they are throwing tantrums all day), and to take a moment to thank God for it.

Maybe it's a simple thing like my son's smile after a long day of seeing his tears.

Or the peace that settles on our home as every one falls asleep.

Or the moments (be they ever so brief) when I catch my kids playing nicely together.

There is something beautiful in every day, we need only to find it, take a breath and enjoy it. The season of life and motherhood passes us by so quickly. I don't want to be so caught up in the difficult that I forget about the beauty.

I may be knee-high in diapers, and my shirt has probably been spit-up on more times than I'd care to count, but motherhood is still a beautiful kind of chaos. We're watching our little ones grow and develop their own personalities and go in their own direction in life.

Motherhood is a beautifully difficult job. Sometimes we focus on the difficult instead of the beauty. Every age has it's difficulties, but every age has its wonderful things about it as well. Sometimes, I have to remind myself to see the amazing through the hard, but it always makes such a difference in our day when I take the time to put my focus where it should be!

What Good Moms Refuse to Admit

So often as moms, we make jokes about what a poor job we must be doing raising our kids. Whether it's the sarcastic laments that the "mother of the year award" must be passing us by after we've just messed something up or the memes about "just trying to keep the kids alive," we're pretty quick to make a joke at our own expense.

I make those jokes, too, and I laugh at them, but I would like to go on record saying I think I'm a good mom. And I bet, if you were honest with yourself, you'd think the same about your own parenting skills. Yes, we're imperfect. I mean, you all know that my children frequently eat chicken nuggets and corn dogs from the freezer, that I RARELY clean my kid's room, that I totally compare my kids to other kids their age, and that I'm secretly relieved when I see other toddlers misbehaving in public.

I am far from being the perfect mom. But really, I'm far from being a terrible mother, too.

That's the whole point is to remind all of us that we don't have to be perfect to be awesome mamas to our kids. We can make mistakes and do things differently than "the norm" and still be fantastic parents to our own children.

So don't be afraid to admit it. **You are a good mom.** Say it loud; say it proud. As loudly as you would say, "I guess the mother of the year award is passing by my house this year," or "I must be the worst mother ever because…"

Be honest with yourself. **Remember your good days, not just your mistakes**. Think about the time you made cookies with your kids or spun in circles until you almost threw up. And if it's been awhile since you've had some silly fun with your kids, don't feel guilty about it -- just schedule something fun for this afternoon, even if it's just an impromptu dance party in the living room. Make them smile, laugh with them. That's all that it takes.

Most importantly, remember...

You are an awesome mom.

Admit it to yourself and don't be afraid to believe it. You are rocking this. And I'm pretty positive you deserve more credit than what you have been giving yourself.

Don't be afraid to be a good mom. Because you already are. Just accept it.

I know there are a lot of good moms reading this right now, so I'm going to ask you to be brave and admit it to yourself.

No disclaimers, not self-deprecating jokes, just remind yourself that you are a good mom to your kids, and think about the fun things you've done recently together.

It doesn't have to be epic or Pinterest-worthy. The most precious memories are often the simplest.

Just take a moment to remind yourself, smile, and go have some more fun with them! You totally deserve it.

Acknowledgements

I feel like I could write an entire book simply thanking people, and while each "thanks" would be truthful and meaningful, it would probably be wearisome to read them all. So, here are just a few of the people in my life who are fabulous and, without whom, this book would not have been completed.

First and foremost, my wonderful husband, Alex. He gave me the time to write, even in the midst of our long days. He encouraged me and remembered to make time for my writing. And he's just all-around awesome.

To my babies, who keep me laughing and inspired me to write our story in this book.

Many thanks to Gabrielle and Becky, for all your critiques, suggestions and red lines. Perhaps one day I will understand how to properly use a comma, but today is (obviously) not that day!

To my wonderful editor Brannan, you took this book and showed me how to make it fantastic. THANK YOU.

To Cindy, for believing in me and encouraging me to keep going, even when I was nervous and ready to throw in the towel (and for being the best mommy-in-law in the world).

To Sarah, for loving my book and making time to read it (and for being such an incredible friend)

To Misty, for being the first person to call me an author, even before my first book had been published.

To Angela, for encouraging me to write an e-book, telling me that I could do it and helping me format it when I was about to cry because of the relentless markup!

To my blog readers, for supporting me along this journey and sticking with me!

To all my many friends and family members not mentioned here for lack of space on the page, not for lack of space in my heart.

And of course, to every one that reads this book, **thank you!** I hope that you have as much fun reading it as I did writing it! Thank you for being there, thank you for your encouragement and love along this journey! Please feel free to contact me via twitter @paula_rollo or on my blog: www.BeautyThroughImperfection.com

Last, and most of all, I'm thankful to God for allowing me to write and to dream. There are so many wonderful things in my life, of which I deserve none, so the privilege to write and make a career out of something that I love is just one of many beautiful examples of His immense love for me. Though it could never compare to the love poured out for me in His death or the bearing of my sins, each gift leaves me in awe. As does the knowledge that, after everything, He still cares for me -- His undeserving child -- and offers me peace.

ABOUT THE AUTHOR

Paula Rollo is a young wife, mama, and writer. Her passions include blogging, hot Houston weather, watching her kids giggle, budgeting, cross stitching and obsessing over Harry Potter, LOTR, and Doctor Who. You can find more of Paula's writing on her blog BeautyThroughImperfection.com, where she writes candidly about her life as a young wife/mama and strives to encourage others in their daily lives.

Made in the USA
San Bernardino, CA
04 August 2015